LARGE PRINT

CONTENTS

VIRUS 5/1/20

MIRACLES HAPPENFOR
YOU, FOR ME

"Read About How My Charitable Donation Created A Miracle, And Miracles Kept Happening."

Excerpts:

> "*$200, I'LL GIVE YOU $300.*"

> "*ARE YOU SURE?*"

> "*BUY MY BUILDING.*"

> "*HOW CAN YOU EAT THIS CRAP?*"

> "*I CAN'T SEE MY HAND.*"

> "*I'VE GOT A BUDDY.*"

> "*WE DON'T NEED THE HORN.*"

Front line fighting

Buchenwald

SCHOOLS DON'T TEACH WHAT YOU WILL READ.

JOE'S UNNATURAL TRUE LIFE EXPERIENCES.

MIRACLES HAPPEN

FOR YOU, FOR ME

This Book is on a Mission, No bull

GOD BLESS AMERICA

Abraham Jospeh Platnick

WHY WOULD YOU WANT
TO READ THIS BOOK?

Because you will see how one man was able to overcome obstacles, even the Federal government.

Read how Joseph Platnick finally stopped the railroad **train horn** at safe crossings in Dade County, Florida. No more trying to, "beat the train".

Also, read how one man, Joe Platnick, as President of Northeast Dade Coalition, with this book, is still trying to convince the Fire Department in Florida that instead of installing sprinklers in residential buildings, to continue with installing electrified smoke detectors, they should be connected to a central alarm system just as a sprinkler system is tied in. He got them to agree to electrifying smoke detectors in lieu of installing sprinklers in high rise residential buildings.

They should also develop a means other than water to extinguish a fire. Water by the Fire department causes more damage to a high rise building than the fire isolated in an apartment.

FIRE OCCURS   הוא?

COMMUNITY AWARENESS FORUM of Del Prado

Joseph Platnick, Pres. 18071 Biscayne Blvd   Aventura, Fl. 33160

305-932-1010 (Tel. & Fax)   e mail: jplatnick@aol.com

FIRE OCCURS - COMPARATIVE INSTALLATION

	ELECTRIFIED SMOKE DETECTORS vs	SPRINKLERS INSTALLED - OLDBLDGS
No one home	Property destroyed	Property partially destroyed
Someone home	Put out quickly: a) smother fire b) bucket of water c) fire extinguisher d) destruction minimal	Property partially destroyed. Fire melts sprinkler head interior. Hot blaze needed.
call 911	Fire squad finds fire mostly out or contained	Fire squad finds fire mostly out or contained
Personnel needed	Fire truck driver and assistant	Fire truck driver and assistant
Comparative cost	$50,000	$1,000,000
Damage to property	Small hole covered by smoke detector	Ceiling ripped open

CONCLUSION:

1- No one home – no loss of life – property damage considerable.
2- Someone home can put out fire once they smell smoke. Almost no damage.
3- Fire would require quick evacuation and sprinkler would go off if fire is intense and there would be major damage.
4- Large fire squad would not be needed in either case. Saves taxpayer's money.
5- An electrician would make a small opening near an electrical outlet for a wire to be connected. The hole would be covered by the detector. Little inconvenience. Not expensive.
6- Ceiling would have to be opened for pipe installation.
   Dirty job, inconvenient to owner, takes a lot of time. Very expensive.

①

Legislation Should require that:

1- The smoke detector be installed by a licensed electrician.

2 - Home shall have a hand held fire extinguisher.

3 - Installer shall explain how to use the fire extinguisher and the smoke alarm test button to the resident in the home.

4 - Fire insurance compnay shall receive diocumentation of installation and that there is a hand held fire extinguisher on the premises whose use was explained to the resident.

5 - With docuemtation that all of the above was carried out, the insurance company shall not increase fire insurance costs as currently contemplated to increase up to 50%.

Smoke Detector mounted on the ceiling

From Wikipedia, the free encyclopedia

"A smoke detector is a device that senses smoke, typically as an indicator of fire. Commercial security devices issue a signal to a fire alarm control panel as part of a fire alarm system, while household smoke detectors, also known as smoke alarms, generally issue a local audible or visual alarm from the detector itself or several detectors if there are multiple smoke detectors interlinked.

Smoke detectors are housed in plastic enclosures, typically shaped like a disk about 150 millimetres (6 in) in diameter and 25 millimetres (1 in) thick, but shape and size vary. Smoke can be detected either optically (photoelectric) or by physical process (ionization); detectors may use either, or both, methods. Sensitive alarms can be used to detect, and thus deter, smoking in areas where it is banned. Smoke detectors in large commercial, industrial, and residential buildings are usually powered by a central fire alarm system, which is powered by the building power with a battery backup. Domestic smoke detectors range from individual battery-powered units, *to several interlinked mains-powered units with battery backup; with these interlinked units, if any unit detects smoke, all trigger even if household power has gone out.*

The risk of dying in a home fire is cut in half in homes with working smoke alarms. The US National Fire Protection Association reports 0.53 deaths per 100 fires in homes with working smoke alarms compared to 1.18 deaths without (2009–2013). Some homes do not have any smoke alarms, some alarms do not have working batteries; sometimes the alarm fails to detect the fire."

*Be sure to check with your local fire department. I assume no responsibility.

<u>*Acknowledgments:*</u>

Thanks to my wife Margo, son Steven, and his wife Kim for their help with the final touches.

Also by Abraham Joseph Platnick:

"Detailed **Index** to the Code of Jewish Law" – (Kitzur Shulchan Aruh)

PROLOGUE

This narrative, which I was inspired to write, may make you think that I am an unusual person. I am not. I went through the motions of life as they occurred beyond my control.

In my opinion, everyone's life is controlled by an outside force, whether we realize it or not. Our Rabbis teach us that we are born with and maintain two inclinations, the good and the bad. It is up to the good to control the bad. We control what actions to take.

Many of my experiences which I describe in this book I have not heard of happening to anyone else. The dates of these occurrences are not necessarily in sequence and I have written about them as they came to my mind.

MYSTICAL EVENT –
MIRROR IMAGE

Could anyone in their wildest imagination have foreseen the event in Stockholm, Sweden, when my wife Margo and I were entering the front door of a train together with other passengers. As I got past the front seats, I saw other passengers in the car getting out of their seats and heading to exit by the middle door. I looked straight at a lady and she looked straight at me. People can live their whole lives and not encounter such an experience.

Margo standing, standing next to me, was astonished. Too bad we did not use our camera before she got off the train with other passengers directly behind her.

We saw a mirror image of my own face!

I still find it hard to believe but Margo was a witness to this. How was this possible? Margo researched and found that the Swedes entered Poland many years ago.

Now I asked Margo, "Do you remember the lady on the train?". "Of course, I remember her". "I'll never forget the resemblance, so perfect!".

THINGS BEYOND MY CONTROL
FREQUENT RELOCATION

How did I manage to grow up? It wasn't easy. I certainly didn't have the normal family upbringing with two loving parents. It was tough making a living for our family of five, and we moved every three years. In those days a landlord would give you three months of concessions and a clean freshly painted apartment for a three-year lease. Naturally, we moved every three years to save on rent, and I never had a chance to make a lasting friendship.

For one of those three-year moves, we landed in Bensonhurst, Brooklyn. It was a nice and mostly Italian neighborhood. We lived in the back of a two-family house. Our Italian lady neighbor was always offering my mother some of the food she'd cooked for her own family, which my mother was embarrassed to accept because we kept strictly kosher and did not know what ingredients were used.

I remember my mother placing kosher meat on a tray and sprinkling it on both sides with kosher salt to remove any vestiges of blood. After an hour or so, she would put the meat in a pail of water for at least a half hour.

MOTHERS' BREAKDOWN

One afternoon, while I was at home, and for some unknown reason, my mother started screaming and waving her arms frantically. After a while, some men came and put her into a straitjacket. As I sat on the outside stoop I started crying while they put my mother into a car and took her away. My father was left to take care of me and my younger brother Bernie.

My father and I moved from there to 642 Willoughby Ave. in Brooklyn. I do not know with whom my brother was staying. I went to public school and was out at 3 P.M. after which I attended Hebrew school until 4:30 P.M. Our Hebrew schoolteacher stood with a 12-inch ruler in his hand he called on different students to read the Hebrew texts. If you didn't know the place within the text to continue, you weren't paying attention and got a splap on the wrist, or "schmeise". My father sent me there in attempt to keep me off of the streets for as much of the day as possible and to keep me out of trouble.

MARCY AVENUE PARK

I used to walk over to Marcy Avenue Park and to play shuffle-board. The fellows were friendly, and I became good friends with one in particular, Bernie Baron. I was good at the game and participated in the park sponsored shuffleboard tournament.

I made my way to the finals and had a game with a tall fellow who was a really good player. It was the final match and I was way behind in points. It looked like I might lose. Suddenly my luck took a turn for the better.

My opponent had a puck in the 8 box, and I had one just touching line. It was my turn to shoot. Wow! I knocked his puck out of the 8 box and into the 10-off box. On the way his puck knocked my loose puck into the 7 box with my shooter remaining in the 8 box. That meant 15 more points for me and 10 points off for him. Even though his score was still ahead, he was so rattled that he couldn't play very well after that. I wound up winning the game and the tournament.

FATHERS' KNITTING MILL

My fathers' knitting mill factory was located in a building located on Grand Street, near the corner of Mulberry Street, in lower Manhattan. In the area commonly known as "Little Italy".

Ferrara's Restaurant was across the street, and Salzberg's machine shop was next door. Jews and Italians always got along great together. Mr. Salzberg even helped me with my invention which I patented, years after I left the Army.

Many days I would travel to Manhattan from Brooklyn Tech and do my homework in his factory's office. Occasionally, after work, my father would take me with him to see a Yiddish show at the theatre on Second Avenue. I once saw the famous comedian Eddie Cantor there. He was great.

LOWER EAST SIDE

My mother's brother, Nathan Bershad, and his family lived on the lower east side of Manhattan. Uncle Nathan had an accident and he was crippled. The City allowed him to open a news stand on the corner of Grand Street and the Bowery (3rd Ave.).

Nathan's son, my cousin Hy, was one month older than me and we were friends. He invited me to join the Henry Street Settlement social club and the "Zombie" gang.

I used to walk from my fathers' factory down Grand Street, say hello to Uncle Nathan, and continue all the way to the lower east side Henry Street Settlement. One day there was an announcement that Eddie Cantor would pay for a two-week vacation at Camp Henry in the Catskills for all the poor tennament kids at the Henry Street Settlement, myself included. We were all so excited over getting to go to camp for two weeks.

The one thing I still remember from my time away at camp was a song we sang about the Tower of London. For posterity's sake, since I don't know if the words are published elsewhere, I am taking the liberty of publishing it here and hope I'm getting it right. When I recite it, I always warn the kids not to get scared. This is a British song with British pronunciation.

ANNE BOLIN SONG

*In the Tower of London, large as life, the ghost of Anne Bolin walks,
I declare. Now Anne Bolin was old King Henry's wife, until 'e 'ad the
eadsman bob 'er 'air.*
*O Yes 'e did a wrong long years ago, and she comes up at night to tell'im
so.*

*With 'er 'ead tucked underneath 'er arm, she waaalks the bloody tower,
With 'er 'ead tucked underneath er arm, at the mid night hour.*

*She comes to old King Henry she means giving him what for.
Gadzooks she means to telling him for having spilt 'er gore.
And just in case the 'eadsman wants to give 'er an encore, she 'as 'er
head tucked underneath 'er arm.*

*Along the drafty corridors for miles and miles she goes.
It's awfully cold there poor Queen its cold there when it blows.
It's awfully hard upon the Queen to have to blow 'er nose, with 'er head
tucked underneath 'er arm.*

*The guards they think it's a football she carries in. And when they've
had a few, they yell, "Is Army going to win." They think its Red Grange
instead of poor old Anne Bolin. With 'er 'ead tucked underneath 'er
arm.*

The 'eadsman cuts the bread and stirs the soup, when in walks Anne Bolin to queer the dew.
She 'olds 'er 'ead up with a wild war whoop, woo-woo, and the 'eadsman cries, please don't drop it in the soup, the soup, the soup.

With 'er 'ead tucked underneath 'er arm, she walks the bloody tower, with 'er 'ead tucked underneath 'er arm at the midnight hour. Boom, Boom.

EARLY EARNINGS

Again, we moved. This time to DeKalb Avenue in Brooklyn. It was during summer recess and I was about 11 years old when the wife of the local grocer on the corner of Throop Avenue passed away. My father got me a job as a helper at the grocery store for $3 per week. My parents said that I should keep the money and put it into a savings account at the Dime Savings Bank down the street. After 10 weeks, I had a bankbook with $30 entered in it.

BAR MITZVAH

Bar Mitzvah time was coming around. I was almost 13 years old and my father started taking me to "shul" with him on Saturday. By that time my mother had a relapse and was back in the hospital, again.

On the way to shul one day we always met a man who offered to tutor me for the upcoming Bar Mitzvah ceremony. The conversation between him and my father usually went something like this...

"How much?" "Too much".

The next week, "How much?", "Too much".

Week after week this went on. Finally, he asked for only $25, but again my father said "Too much", so no lessons.

On the day of my Bar Mitzvah I went up to the alter, or "beema", and said the mandatory prayers, which were easy. However, someone else had to continue with the "Haftorah" which I should have done if I'd had taken the lessons. After services, my father celebrated with offering everyone cookies and schnapps. That was my great Bar Mitzvah.

When my brother got Bar-Mitzvah-ed, my mother was home, and my father made an elaborate celebration. I'm pretty sure that my brother got lessons, but I turned out more religious today.

STARTING OUT

I was born 1925 and have a brother who's 3 years younger and a sister who's 10 year younger than me. My father came from Lublin, Poland and my mother, who was a terriffic cook as I remember, came from Bessarabia, Hungary. Upon coming to America, my father spent six months in school to learn English, but at home we always spoke Yiddish.

My father tried various jobs in order to make a living. He learned to be a hand knitter, and along with his partners Adler and Myrowitz started their own knitting mill (Pladmor). My father bought them out and built up the business.

When I was about ten, it was during the great depression. I tried saving stamps and soon went on to comic books. I had about 3 Capt. Marvel books when I asked my mother for my monthly 10 cents allowance so that I could get another book. Her reply," I haven't got it".

We lived in an apartment house in Williamsburg, Brooklyn, New York. I went to Junior High School 148 for one year. I was good in math, always being the first one in a class of 48 to come up with the correct answer to a problem on the blackboard. At graduation, the teacher suggested that I apply for Brooklyn Technical High School. I passed the math test and was admitted. Four difficult years ensued, but it was worth it. I took the mechanical engineering course at Brooklyn Tech and learned to use all kinds of tools, higher mathematics, mechanical drawing, etc.

GROWING UP

We couldn't afford the things people take for granted today. No home phone, no bicycle, no baseball glove (we played with a tennis ball and a broom stick in the street).

Every day, after school, as a teenager, I went to my fathers' factory. I helped in the factory and started to learn how the knitting machines operated. After a while, if a machine broke down, I would fix it.

WORLD WAR II

Brooklyn Tech was an all boy's school. World War two was in full bloom when I graduated, and I was drafted into the army. Again, all boys.

When I graduated from Brooklyn Tech, I had a choice of enlisting in the Army or the Air Corp. My father suggested that I stay out as long as possible. Two weeks later I got my draft notice for the Army, so no choice.

I went to boot camp for three months basic training where we were put physically into shape and learned the use of a few types of firearms.

I didn't eat the food at bootcamp because I kept kosher. All I would eat were the waffles and I was losing strength. After two weeks I wrote and told my father. He wrote back and said that the Rabbis give permission to eat non-kosher food if nothing else was available, "but you don't have to enjoy it". So, I started eating, but avoided the non-kosher meats. These days I keep kosher, not only for religious and health reasons, but I think of my mother being very scrupulous in that respect.

Three months of basic training where we learned the use of all kinds of weapons. I made expert in mortar.

With bootcamp completed, I got on a troop ship, regularly just a freighter, and sailed for France, which took 3 weeks. I landed at the french port city of Le Havre, which had been completely flattened in the D-Day invasion. Not a wall was standing in the whole city. I couldn't believe the devastation.

I was assigned as number-two man in a machine gun squad. When I told the Captain (Jewish name) that I made expert in mortar, he replied "We don't need anyone in mortar!". The squad didn't like the idea that I replaced the number-two man. When these southerners found out that I was Jewish, they looked for horns. They told me that the Germans harmed Jews. My dog tag had an "H" stamped on it, for Hebrew. I threw it into some nearby bushes.

I was with the 87th Infantry, Company H. The bulge was just about over, and we were moving between Belgium and Luxemburg every few days and always at night. Before I left the states, I heard that my cousin Hy Bershad, a month older than me, was wounded at the bulge with shrapnel throughout his body and will be in a hospital in France for months. He didn't spend 5 years attending high school which I was required to do in order to graduate, so he was draft earlier than me.

In Belgium I was told to stand guard over some barren ice-covered land. I had to stand hours in a fox hole. After a while we came to a town in Belgium which was swarming with American soldiers. When the Sargent of our machine gun squad said to "Fall out". I ran to one of the houses surrounding the square we were in, ran up the stairs, jumped into a bed near the window, another GI jumped on top of me, and I got ready to get some sleep. Should I take off my shoes or leave them on? It was freezing in the house and we kept our clothes on. I decided to take off my shoes. When I awoke, my right foot was swollen. I could not put on my shoe, so I put on my golashes and went to the medical people. They sent me to a hospital. I think it was in Reims, France.

I was put onto a cot with many other cots lined up on both sides of me and cots across the aisle. I was covered with a sheet except for my feet. Across the aisle I saw a soldier with a black foot and no other foot. I considered myself lucky.

After one month in the hospital I rejoined my squad. I became last man.

We were ready to attack. We were just 8 men, 6 carrying 50 pounds of 50 caliber bullets in 2 containers, one for each hand, the front two were the gunners.

WE LED THE WAY

It's night and we are waiting for orders to move forward. Our goal is to capture five towns. At around midnight we moved forward. We crossed a narrow shallow stream by walking single file across railroad tiles barely above the water line. When we got to the other side, at our left a machine gun started shooting and I could see the flames. I jumped into a culvert for water drainage at the right side of the road, looked straight up and said, "If I come out alive, I won't work on Shabbos". Then someone at our left yelled out, "We got him". I got up and we moved out, not knowing what to expect. We kept moving. There was no opposition.

By the time we got to the third town it was daylight and people in the houses to our left were opening their second-floor shutters and looking down at us. Suddenly we see a car coming towards us. We set up the machine gun and stopped the car. Inside were a German officer and two German soldiers. They were unarmed. The officer was on his way to visit his wife in the second town. One man of our squad walked them back to where our troops were.

We continued unopposed until we came to the last house and barn of the fifth town. A small doorway at the right of the barn, which was next to a house, was standing a goat. The house at the right had its door open showing a beautiful kitchen. The wall cabinets had doors with a key in each lock. We met the woman of the house, no one else. Looking at the goat I said to myself that we haven't had any milk for months. Maybe I can milk the goat. I tried, but the goat kept jumping around. Finally, the woman came out with some food in a small dish and another bowl. While the goat ate, she milked the goat. Got very little and offered it to me. I reached with my finger and then stopped. I said to the woman that you need it more than me.

We started on our track through Germany. All I knew was that we were headed to Chekoslovakia to meet the Russians.

Along the six month walk we encountered fire from two mortar shells. We replied with our machine gun to some movement on a hill nearby, and the people fled. We continued with no opposition except in Boppard when we had to cross a stream.

One day we encountered machine gun fire from the other side. Therefore, we moved out at night and crossed elsewhere. Another night we walked on a very narrow path alongside a steep mountain dotted with six-foot poles scattered above and below us. Probably wine country.

Finally, we got a ride on a jeep and followed the one in front. We came to the end of the road and had to turn right or left. I watched as the people in the front jeep took out a map. One said, "which way?" "I don't know, let's go left." "OK." We came to the top of a hill. Looking down we could see the town of Plauen completely flattened. A fire was still burning to the left of the town's center. The town square was filled with women, not a child nor a man. We came down to the square and another squad came into town opposite us with a German police officer and two soldiers. When they came to us, I frisked then. The officer had a small pistol. I asked my buddies "Who wants it?". They replied "Joe, you keep it", which I did.

HELLO COUSIN HY

The war was practically over at that time. We went to a very large grassy field and a sign with Company H in front of us. Surprisingly I had recieved a letter from my father back home. It said that my "cousin Hy was discharged from the hospital and had rejoined his unit, the 87th Infantry, Company .... What?" I went looking for him. "HELLO HY".

Can you imagine? In the middle of a war and near its end, deep in Germany. Then someone said that we were to go into the woods with white flags and tell the Germans that the war was over. I yelled out, "Are you crazy, we went all through Germany and now you want us to get killed?" We didn't go, thank G-d.

We moved to a small area next to a forest and with a barn. We were to wait there two weeks for the Russians.

A FOREST NEXT TO US

Let's go see the movies in the barn. We waited for the first group to come down and then we went up. We saw movies for a half hour of the German soldiers killing defenseless people, after first having them dig their own graves. Men, women and children. It was horrible. When we came back down, I asked where we'd gotten these films. From the prisoners of war. What were they going to do with them? They were going to "send them to their families."

BUCHENWALD

We were asked, "Who wants to visit a castle and who wants to visit Buchenwald?" What's Buchenwald?

I don't know but some Jews are there. I said that I'll go to Buchenwald. "But you will have to wait a week while we clean it up."

WARNING: THE FOLLOWING PARAGRAPHS ARE ABOUT BUCHENWALD AND IS NOT PLEASANT READING. YOU MAY WISH TO SKIP THEM.

You know the story in Europe up until Buchenwald. This was an encounter I didn't expect. The week went by, a few of us got into the back of a truck and we drove about a half hour. We stopped at a high metal fence and above a double doorway was a sign which read, ARBEIT MACHT FREI (work makes you free). The double gate swung open and we drove inside. Immediately I smelled death. I never smelled it before, but I knew what it was. At my left I saw a man in a striped uniform standing on a high stoop in front of a door leading into a building. He had a swollen stomach. I thought to myself that he must eat well.

We then stopped at another building and were guided inside. We saw wooden shelves about 6-foot-long and about 15 feet deep, about 10 inches apart, from floor to ceiling which was high. We were told that 15 people would sleep on a shelf. The wall was lined with shelves. We were also told that 2,500 people slept in that room. There was one toilet at the far end of the room.

After the war I met Julie Ross, a concentration camp suvivor, at Congregation Ohr Torah in N. Woodmere, N.Y. Julie told me that if you were on a lower shelf you were bound to get wet.

When I moved to Plaza Del Prado in Miami, Florida I met a fellow GI from the 87th Infantry, Al Schoenberg, who was with the squad which liberated Buchenwald. He asked me if I saw the piles of bodies. What happened to the Germans? "O, they ran".

On my own I walked to another building. Inside I walked up a ramp at my left. As I walked up, I looked down in a large pit. On the far wall to my right were semicircular grooves inside the wall. About 8 of them about a foot apart. I believe there was a metal stretcher at the far end of the room.

A large high window was to my left and there was a railing at my right to prevent me from falling down. As I walked, I came upon two men in striped uniforms talking to each other. Then I heard them speaking Yiddish which I also spoke. We got into a conversation and then one of the men said, "When the arm is sticking out, I chop it off and throw it on top of the body," I got sick and got out of there fast.

I then walked to another building, looked inside, very high ceiling, with what looked like a couple of sprinkler heads on top.

We then got back to the truck and went back to camp.

At camp, I was assigned guard duty on a narrow road in the forest. The road turned left and after a while I went to the end of the road and looked left. A short distance away were some Russian soldiers. One had on a cap with a red star at the top. I continued my stroll and I began to realize that I had gone for months all through Germany and never shot my gun once. I don't know where I got the material, but I made a target, put it up on a tree, and from far away, shot a bull's eye. After a while a German kid comes up to me. He asked me "what was that shot about?". I showed him my bulls' eye and he left. That started me thinking. Is it possible that the people living in the town next to Buchenwald didn't know what was going on?

TRANSFERRED TO THE
90TH INFANTRY

L ater on, I was transferred to the 90th Infantry. I was told that cousins should not be in the same outfit. The 90th was in occupation. The 87th was going to Japan. I didn't complain. One day we were lined up for target practice. We faced silhouettes and were told that this was rapid fire. Whoever got twelve shots on target got a trip to Paris. After we finished shooting, the officer came up to me. You got 11 and the 12th cracked the side of the paper. Let me see if the Captain will issue you a pass. I said, "never mind, I've been to Paris after the hospital."

Anyway, we were deep into Germany, I had no idea where, and I had no money. We stayed in this town for a while and then we shipped out, heading to Japan. When we got to England, I got a pass to visit London. At Piccadilly Circus I went into a restaurant and was the only one there. I sat on a stool at the counter and a waitress came to me with a menu. I said what I wanted. We haven't got it. I chose something else. We haven't got it. I chose something else. We haven't got it. I put down the menu, what have you got? Fish and chips. OK. Then we heard hollering and screaming outside the window near us. Looking outside we saw people dancing and jumping on top of cars. What's going on? Japan surrendered! Couldn't be better news.

GOOD OLD USA

Getting back to the States was a lot more comfortable than going to Europe. Three days on the Queen Mary. Couldn't wait to get home. Came into the army camp in New Jersey and told we had a 2-week pass. If we invited anyone to the mess hall, we had to get a pass. I called my brother Bernie to pick me up and I got a pass for him. When he arrived, we went for lunch. It was cafeteria style. We got in line behind the counter, handed our plate to the fellow on the other side, and I said, "give me some of that some of that, some of that, some of that, etc." When my brother sat down next to me at the table, I said to him, "Isn't this great?" He looked at me and said, "How can you eat this crap?"

RETURNING G.I.'S

I didn't belong to any particular Army outfit and was transferred to different camps. I was waiting to accumulate enough points to be discharged. At one camp, since I could understand German a little, so the Captain asked me to stay with the German prisoners of war who were sorting out the clothing into different bins the G I's coming from Japan were discarding.

One day the head German comes to me with a piece of paper. Can you figure out this mathematical problem? I saw he was trying to put me down. Well, he got the shock of his life. I gave him the answer right then and there. He went screaming back to where the other Germans were working yelling that I figured it out. I should have told him that I was Jewish. That really would have made his day.

DISCHARGED

Finally, I got my discharge and started to go with my father to work in his factory. I said to my father, "Not me." His replied "Why not? We always go in on Saturday." I told him my pledge in the war. After I told him what happened, he put up his right hand and said, "Don't go. But I have the keys and I have to open up." From then on, I don't think he opened on Saturday.

My fathers' factory produced 600 dozen sweaters per week during the season which lasted about 9 months. One day I went into his office and checked the payroll. It was during the slow season and he was shipping 300 dozen a week. I noticed that his payroll was the same as if he shipped 600 dozen. I went to him and told him what I found. He couldn't believe it until I showed him the figures. I suggested that he is better off closing shop during the off season. He agreed and we saved thousands every week.

COLLEGE

I heard about Public Law 16 and getting a college education. I went to take the test. Alone in this small room with a young fellow sitting at a small folding table. He gave me the test sheet to fill out while we were sitting there. I finished the thirty questions, no problem. He looked at me and said, "Any college you want, for as long as you want, and free books". I was not smart enough to realize what he told me. I knew my father wanted me in the factory, so I chose NYU which was in Manhattan and I could commute easily. My father had a good accountant who made a good living and my father always said that I should either become a knitting machine mechanic or an accountant.

At NYU I chose the accounting course. I went to class. There must have been over 100 students in the room. I got a seat in the last row. The teacher gave 2 questions to one long row and another 2 questions to the next row. I am about to answer these two questions which were no problem to me when the guy sitting next to my right started bugging me to help him with his questions. He kept nudging me constantly and I couldn't write the answers to my questions. I forgot what the questions were until we were ready to leave the room and I remembered the second question which I immediately wrote the answer, leaving the other question blank. Coming to class the next day I got a 50 and the "noodge" got 70. He said that he was sorry.

I never went back to school. I became a knitting machine mechanic. My wife Margo is reviewing this writing and she just said that if I went to Harvard we would probably not have met.

MET MARGO

Around this time, circa 1945-1946, during the weekends, I would walk over to Marcy Avenue Park and play shuffleboard. I became friendly with a fellow named Bernie Baron. I was working for my father at the time, while Bernie Baron got a revered job with the U.S. Post Office. One day he suggested that we go to a dance in Rego Park at a synagogue. I drove there in my fathers' old jalopy. A band was playing.

At the dance, I saw a group of girls and a tall girl stood out. I asked for a dance. (As part of being discharged from the Army, we were taught how to dance.) We got friendly and I offered to drive her home after the dance. She accepted and Bernie said to go ahead, he will manage to get home. When she refused to go in the back seat, I knew she was for me. We got married a year later at her suggestion.

I became friendly with her father who was widowed a year earlier. Margo and Sigmund Hopfenmaier invited me to join them for meals. We told jokes. He was in business selling a variety of things and Margo, who graduated City College at a tremendous total cost of $76 and even resold her used books, would help him.

Margo also became friendly with my father and visited his factory often, even selling sweaters for him. We are still together, thank G-d. Margo and her parents were luckily thrown out of Germany before the war. That's another story.

REPAIR KNITTING MACHINES

One day my father suggested that in order for me to get more experience I should get a job in a different factory. Who will hire me? "I'll get you a job." Sure enough, my father got me a job in another mill with 4 circular Jacquard knitting machines, all of which were just standing there out of commission. I was offered a salary of $150 per week, with no work on Saturday. What a boost from $25 that my father paid me.

After a year I had all my employers' machinery running perfectly. I had $5,000 in my bank account. I was single, living with my father, and no expenses except for going to a Catskill Mountain Hotel for the weekend. Then my father called me. "I need your help. My machines are broken down and if you don't help me, I'll probably have to go out of business." What could I do? I had to give notice to my boss. When I told my boss the situation, he said that the machines were working fine, and I can go help my father. I also went back to $25 a week. I got my fathers' machines working fine and got another job elsewhere for $200 a week.

I switched jobs again, this time to a used machinery dealer – Steinberg Brothers. My job was to set up machines in different factories and teach the people how they operated. Steinberg also started importing machinery from Germany. He was selling machinery to factories with lower wage scales, gradually going south of New York as far as Puerto Rico.

Going into different mills I saw a separating machine which made it easier for a girl to pull out nylon threads from between the cloth. However, the thread would break in the middle. I came up with the use of a slipping clutch as is used on a fishing reel. Steinberg had no objection to me selling these improved machines.

I also had an idea for an invention to make designs in the fabric while the machine was knitting its' regular fabric. I also had a chance to import machinery and maybe start my own knitting mill.

While working for Steinberg, I was sent to a mill to set up a Brinton machine. When I was about to leave, the boss comes over to me. "My mechanic died last week, and he couldn't fix this Jacquard machine. Could you?" He showed me the problem and I said, "No big deal". The boss said, "But my mechanic couldn't fix it". I said that It won't take me long. The boss replied, "I want you to call the Jacquard Company and get instructions". I told him there was "No need." He insisited that we call Jacquard. The call wen something like this:

"Hello, is this the Jacquard Company." "Yes".

"May I speak to Joe Tytell?"

"Speaking."

"I have a man here who is to fix one of your machines."

"Put him on. (The boss is listening.) Whom am I speaking to?"

"Joe Platnick".

"Joe, leave me alone, you know what to do." (He hangs up.)

I loosened the bolts holding the automat, put it one gear notch into position, fastened the bolts, and tried it out. No good. Loosened the bolts, moved the automat gear 2 notches in the opposite direction, fastened the bolts. Tried it out. Fixed perfectly. The boss is watching. Astonished. Maybe you can fix this other machine which is occasionally breaking needle butts inside the cams." "I will look at it". After poking at protruding needle heads around the machine. I said to the young man who has been hanging around me all the time that I was there, "Please take off these 2 sections". He took them off. I turned them upside down. "There's your problem, one of the cams is sticking out too far. I proceeded to grind the cam to its proper shape, put it back into the section. I told the kid to put back on the secitons we'd removed. Which he did. The boss came over and asked the kid "Did he fix it?". The kid nodded yes. The boss looked at me and asked how much Steinberg was paying me, I told him $200 a week. He instatly made me an offer; "Come work for me, I will give you $300" (in 2020 dollars that would be equivalent to over $4,300 a week), "and you can keep selling your separating machines." I kindly refused his offer "No, Steinberg needs me". But like I said, I had other plans in mind.

GOING FISHING WEEKLY

Now that Margo and I are married, we started looking for a place to live even though my father-in-law, Sigmund, offered his bedroom. As a GI we were able to get an apartment in Northridge, a development in Queens, not far from Sigmund.

Shortly after we moved in, we parking our car in the underground garage. Another car pulled into a nearby space and a fellow with some fishing rods got out of his car. Strangely I had just bought a fishing rod, so I got into a conversation with Bobby Nestler. I showed him how flexible my rod was, and as I bent it, it broke in half. I was so embarrassed and I didn't know what to do. Bobby was very cool. He said, "Don't worry, I'll get you a new rod." And he did.

It so happened that Bobby was my neighbor on the same floor. We started going fishing together. Neither of us were religious, and we went every Saturday on party boats throughout New York and Long Island. It was very relaxing for me. Bobby suggested that we buy a 10-horsepower outboard motor so that we could rent a rowboat out on the island. We shared the cost of the motor and other expenses. It was great. We went every week, rain or shine, winter or summer. We dressed accordingly. A successful night's fishing trip brought me and Bobby a potato sack full of Bluefish.

I dumped the fish into the bathtub and when Margo got up- she screamed. I came into the room and calmed her down. Later that night I met Bobby. "What did you do with all the fish?" I asked. He told me, "I went next door to Mrs. Nussbaum and asked her if she would like some fresh blue fish". Mrs. Nussbaum asked "Is it Kosher?" I repled, "Yes, of course it's kosher". She said "OK, give me a slice".

LEARNED "ROBERTS RULES OF ORDER"

Somehow, I cannot remember exactly, I met a fellow named Dave Schoenfeld, who was coincidentally also a fisherman. Dave got me into the Knights of Pythias. We had great meetings, card games, movies for which I did not stay. Margo was waiting for me; I didn't need movies.

After a few years I became the Chancellor Commander. I had to conduct the meetings strictly in accordance with Roberts Rules of Order. If I made a mistake, the Past Chancellors would hassle me. I studied the book carefully and didn't make a mistake.

That year we put $300 into a special account so that the Grand Lodge wouldn't take our money. The Secretary got sick so some of the Past Chancellors went to the bank to find out how much we had accumulated. He found that the $300 we'd stashed away was missing and the account was emptied The Secretary had his brother-in-law co-sign a blank check. The Secretary died shortly thereafter. I, if no one else, learned a lesson.

GOING INTO BUSINESS

I said to Margo that I cannot work in my fathers' factory with my brother Bernie and my brother-in-law who both contributed their talents to the business. It was a union shop and the wages could not compete with the non-union shops in Ridgewood, Queens run by Germans. I explained that the only way I could leave and in order to be on my own, was if I go into my own business.

At this time, I got involved importing knitting machines from Germany. I made a lot of improvements but one problem I could not overcome. The cams were controlled electrically, and the switches used would break down too frequently. I imported and sold a few machines to people who could handle them. I got stuck with 3 machines which I placed in a store in Oceanside, not far from the house we just bought in Valley Stream with the money Margo's father left her recently.

I installed my invention on two of the machines and started making sample sweaters. Every day that I wasn't making samples, I would go around to different Jobbers with my sample case loaded. I kept doing this and I was getting nowhere. It was very frustrating, and I was ready to give up and get a job.

AND THEN, A MIRACLE HAPPENED

In the meantime, we were able to adopt a son, Steven, also given the Hebrew name of Margo's father, Issachar.

Next door to our house at 115 Brookside Drive, Valley Stream, moved in Rabbi Dr. Theodore Jungreis, his wife Esther, and their 2 sons and 2 daughters. We became friendly and he suggested that I get a copy of the Code of Jewish Law, which I did. That is another story.

One day, while raking up the fallen leaves in my back yard, I see the Rabbi doing the same. He called me over to the fence and said that he is the Rabbi at the nearby Young Israel Synagogue. Some people heard him speak at the shul and since they are starting a new community in North Woodmere, would he be their Rabbi? He asked me, "What should he do?". I said, "You have to go. It will be a Jewish Community and if you don't go, they may get a Rabbi who isn't Orthodox." I was asked over the fence if I would also contribute a thousand dollars as others have pledged? Of course, I said yes.

I don't know if he took my advice or someone else's, but I got a call to come to a meeting in a house in North Woodmere. I went. The house was packed. People standing on the steps leading up. Then the Rabbi and his wife entered the house. There was the usual routine and then they asked Mayor of Valley Stream, Sy Morgenroth, who lived a few houses down the street from where we lived, to be the President. He couldn't refuse. Then they asked me to be the treasurer. Of course, I could not refuse, even though I wasn't making a living at the time.

After the meeting I asked a lady named Laura Epstein where I should open a bank account. Laura said, "Anywhere on Rockaway Avenue". At 9 A.M. the next morning I went with my suitcase to a bank on Rockaway Avenue. The clerk at the desk asked me if he could help me. I said that I would like to open a new account. He replied, "Fine, I'll be right back", and walked away. I said to myself, how I can open an account, nobody gave me any money. But those days I always carried a blank check. I took it out of my wallet and made it out for $1,000 and left the bank.

My first stop after opening the account at the bank was to try and get an order. For three months I'd been knocking on doors with no success. I introduce myself to the fellow behind the desk, open my sample case, and he gives me an order for 200 dozen sweaters. I couldn't believe it. I said, "Are you sure?". He said "yes". He put me in business. Congregation Ohr Torah put me in business! From then on, I kept improving the business. There is no limit as to what tzedakah can do. To this day, I do not spare donations. But always "know to whom you give" (quote from the Ethics of Our Fathers).

MORE MIRACLES

My business really took off once I moved to 2071 Fulton Street near Rockaway Ave in Brooklyn. It was a factory building built maybe 100 years before and housed heavy machinery requiring heavy electrical wiring.

There was a fireplace on the first floor with a brick chimney going up through the second and third floors. The rear of the building was at 48 Somers Street. The freight elevator was large, and you had to pull a cable either up or down in order to get it moving. I took possession of half of the third floor. Coal was used to heat the building.

When I moved there, it was an Italian neighborhood with a large grocery at one side of the building and a small meat store on the other side. We were near the corner subway station and there was lots of bus traffic.

It was no problem getting people to work for me. I trained them to do work as if I were at Brooklyn Tech. I made sure there was adequate aisle space for the flow of the sweaters we made and for emergency exit. Almost all our employees were paid piece work, so we knew of a steady production. No fooling around. Lots of compliments. Very friendly atmosphere.
Margo came to work in my factory once it started producing. She was the designer and salesperson. Without her I could not have been successful. We worked 50 weeks a year with 2 weeks paid vacation. We were successful for five years and something new happened. We had a surprise visitor.

ANOTHER SURPRISE

Entering the third floor of the building a man says, "Hello, my name is Mr. Oberlander, I'm the owner of this building. Is Mr. Platnick here?". I answered, "Yes, I am Platnick. What can I do for you?". The usual greetings took place and then Mr. Oberlander said that he asked the tenant on the first floor if he would be interested in buying his building but he had said no. He also had asked the tenant on the second floor who also said no. He asked me if I would I be interested. This was a surprise. Thinking quickly, I began to surmise what could happen if he sold the building to someone else who would make me move. I would lose two weeks of production plus moving costs. How much is involved? I asked Mr. Oberlander, "How much are you asking?". He replied, "$15,000 down and the rest we can negotiate, but it will be reasonable".

I said, "OK, you've got a deal". We shook hands. "Here comes my wife. Margo, I'd like you to meet Mr. Oberlander. He just sold us this building."

I didn't know what to expect. After Mr. Oberlander left, I explained my thinking and she agreed. But, by buying the building, not knowing anything about construction, I immediately started learning. Not only did I have my growing business on my hands, but many needed repairs to the building.

Thank G-d, we did good business for 6 years, 50 weeks of the year with two weeks paid vacation to all employees. We had 25 happy employees who were very friendly to each other. We tried to produce on an assembly line strategy and the goods flowed steadily, 200 dozen sweaters a week. I taught the operators how to get all sewing-seams perfectly straight. We avoided shipping anything damaged and in a year, we only had 6 sweaters as returns. That is considered remarkable in the industry. After all, I am a Brooklyn Tech graduate.

Things are going along great in business with Margo taking care of the designing and sales while I did the machinery and building repairs, when in walks another surprise visitor, the local Assemblyman. He introduced himself and asked for a $100 donation to the Democratic Club. I gave him a check. First time he ever came around. Yes, there was something else on his mind.

"Mr. Platnick, we would like to rent this entire building. We want to establish a Day Care Center."

"Why my building?"

"Because it is the only large building near a subway stop and two bus lines."

"I'm sorry but I have my business here."

He came back the following month for another check with the same request to rent our building. Again, I gave him a check and told him "sorry, no rental". Later in the day Margo said that a lot of owners of buildings are going into renting Day Care Centers, that I should go downtown and look into it. I did as she requested and since we saw that the sweater market was being taken over by Japanese imports, that it might be a good idea to sell out.

AGAIN A SURPRISE

We told the local Assemblyman that we would go along with his idea. We got a City of New York backed lease, an architect and a contractor who was very good. We were lucky. We got a mortgage for $650,000.

NEGOTIATING A CITY LEASE

One of the contentions we had when negotiating the lease with the city people was the use of our elevator and the city's leases typically only undertook the maintenance of a dumbwaiter. The negotiators in our case would not assume the cost of maintaining the elevator which was used for food transport. We knew that other Centers used dumbwaiters to bring food up to the classrooms from the basement kitchen and the City maintained the dumbwaiters.

As we sat at a table in the basement arguing this point, I suddenly slumped forward on my face. I passed out. Margo told me later that she was raising my arms frantically. An ambulance crew arrived. I awoke and looked around, saying, "Where am I? Who are you? (The city negotiators were just standing there doing nothing) Why did you wake me from such a wonderful dream?" (I dreamt of being in a flower garden.)

Margo is continuing what happened to me:

The ambulance dispatcher sent Joe to a local doctor as they felt that it was not an emergency. The doctor checked out Joe and advised to see a specialist, a neurologist in Seattle. We contacted a neurologist, the specialist in Seattle, who recommended Dr. Ramsay, whom he went to school with, at Jackson Memorial Hospital in Miami.

We flew home and Joe was admitted to Jackson Memorial. A pacemaker was immediately installed.

<u>Thank you Margo.</u>

MIAMI HERE I COME

My aching back. The cold winters in New York were no good to me. We decided to move to Miami, Florida. We found a nice condominium that was only three years old. A two-bedroom, two baths, and reasonably priced, so we bought it. We became snowbirds, driving back and forth to New York. In Florida I joined the Jewish War Veterans and became friendly with the Commander. Meeting attendance was sparse, so we started inviting interesting speakers on local topics. Attendance improved considerably.

The condo we bought in is called Plaza Del Prado. It is located on Biscayne Blvd and N.E. 180th Street. Biscayne Blvd. (U.S.1) which was 2 lanes North and 2 lanes South. I was asked to be a member of the Dade County Citizens Transportation Advisory Committee (CTAC). When it was proposed that Biscayne Blvd. be widened, I suggested that land on the west side be used. That's where 3 special houses were located. A project managers' name was published in the newspaper and meeting place was given. I went there and so did some people from neighboring condos such as Commodore Plaza and Admirals Port. After speaking to the manager, the few of us left and I nonchalantly said, "You know that we condominiums have a lot in common. Why don't we get together?". They thought it a great idea, so we made plans and met. They made me the President. We met monthly. A CPA, Mr. Levy, living at Commodore, became our treasurer and our dues were $25 per year. We were all volunteers. Our members were either the President or Manager of the affilaited condominimums. We called the organization the Northeast Dade Coalition and had, after four years, 85 Condominium Members. Attendees were Presidents and managers of the condo. We would have an interesting speaker and a sponsor who paid for refreshments, gave out literature, and spoke for 5 minutes. We usually had about 100 people attend each meeting. Then I decided to give the Presidency over to others. Two people, Patricia and Paul Libert, took over. Their accomplishment was to get a state law passed that required new members of a condominium board of directors be taught the Florida laws for condominiums. They increased the membership.

AVENTURA

While I was President, I met with Senator Gwen Margolis and the developer of the Aventura Shopping Center in my apartment kitchen. They asked about giving this new city, which we just started, a name. They suggested Aventura. That was the same name as the developer's shopping center. I said that I have nothing better. So, we decided to call the city Aventura.

FLORIDA AS HOME

When we moved into our Florida apartment I felt at home. I put on a yarmulke (skullcap). This building was a condominium and we contributed monthly maintenance. When I left the apartment, I still felt like I was at home, so I wore the yarmulke. I was paying taxes for the area around the condo, so shouldn't I wear a yarmulke off premises? Why not? Forty years ago, I was the only man that I saw wearing a yarmulke on the streets. I was never harassed or embarrassed. I wore my yarmulke at all public and political functions and meetings and was never embarrassed. I still wear a yarmulke everywhere I go. I say hello to anyone I meet.

But, according to Jewish law, I am not allowed to touch anyone of the opposite sex but my wife or child. Maybe that would be a good law for everyone to follow, including not being alone in a room with a strange person of the opposite sex unless the door is open to a busy corridor.

Another unusual incident. A few days after moving here I was driving east on Miami Gardens Drive (MGD) near W. Dixie Highway and saw a policeman giving a ticket to a man in the corner shopping center. I was new here and wasn't familiar with the laws. I want to avoid a ticket, so I drove onto the shopping center lot, got out of my car, went over to the policeman, and asked what the driver did wrong. He said that he went forward on the right lane of MGD when he should have made a right turn. It is a right turn only lane. I thanked the policeman and left. When I got home, I called the traffic department and spoke to a traffic engineer. I explained the location, said that very few cars make a right turn at that corner, and if he would check it out. I left my phone number. A few days later he calls me up and thanks me for the information. They are going to change it to go straight. It gives them an extra lane. I think it must have been shortly after that, when I was asked to be a member of Citizen's Transportation Advisory Committee (CTAC). I also got involved with the traffic lights. Whenever there was a pileup, I would call Frank at traffic lights and tell him. He thanked me because he is stuck behind his desk. I was asked to volunteer to be a member of the CTAC and I accepted. We had monthly meetings at City Hall.

Margo got after me. "You've got to get involved in something". "But I'm looking to invest our money so we could have an income". We have been going to the library and studying the stock and bond monthly books and the Industrial Survey book. I made a vow that if Hashem helps me, I will work as a volunteer for the community.

"Leave me alone."

"No, I want you to get a Real Estate License."

"I want you to go to Gold Coast School." "OK, I'll go to school."

I went to school and got my license. I still worked as a volunteer and didn't get a job. Then Margo says that I should become a Broker. I went back to school and became a broker. I printed up business cards but didn't bother with that either. I'm just not a good salesman.

SAVED A LIFE

Shortly after moving into Del Prado Condominium in Florida, I was walking in the lobby and passed a room at my right filled with people. I stood in the doorway and watched a demonstration of giving mouth to mouth resuscitation to someone on the floor. Then the volunteer was seated up on the floor and the teacher showed how to do the Heimlich Maneuver, which is the teacher getting behind the seated volunteer on the floor, reaching his arms around the back of the volunteer, making a fist with his two hands, and pulling his hands hard into the abdomen of the volunteer, a few times. Then putting the victim back flat on the floor and continuing with mouth to mouth, holding the victims' nose.

The reason I am bringing this up is because a few years later, while at a dinner party, I saved a man's life doing the above when no one else stepped forward to help the man who passed out. "His color is coming back". He sat up on the floor. 9-1-1 then arrived.

BACK PAIN

Even in Florida I was suffering with severe back pain. The chiropractor here didn't help. The Veterans Administration (VA) authorized special shoes, but that didn't help. Going to the local Parkway Hospital they said that I had spinal stenosis and I needed an operation. What can be done? I couldn't even drive our car. On a Jewish holiday we went to the Crown Hotel. While taking a walk with Margo on the boardwalk, two friends called me over.

"Joe, you look like you're in terrible pain."

"I sure am."

"Why don't you do what we did?"

"What did you do?"

"We went to the pain clinic."

"So what?"

"We used to be in wheelchairs."

"Tell me about it."

"This hospital has a pain clinic. You go at 9 A.M. until 4:30 P.M. There are no pills nor shots, just exercise. You go for one month every day. That's all."

The next morning, with all my x-rays, I was at the hospital. They examined my x-rays and said that they think they can help me. Margo worked for the Federal Government, so we had good insurance. Margo drove me there every morning and took me home at night. After two weeks of specific exercises, I was able to drive the car. After a month, I was able to speed walk. No jogging. I was able to walk a mile and a half, to and from Skylake Synagogue every Saturday morning. No pain. I continue to this day with a series of exercises every day. Today I use a walker because I get dizzy and am afraid to fall and my legs start hurting after a short walk. For a long walk I use a wheelchair. Thank G-d Margo helps me.

TRAIN HORN

Returning to Florida, I was greeted by the usual Florida East Coast (FEC) train horn. People were complaining but no one was doing anything about it. Why a train horn in Florida and not in New York? Surprisingly I got a call from Mayor John Cavalier, Jr. of Miami Springs.

"I understand that you want to do something about the train horn."

"Yes"

"Will you help me?"

"Yes".

"Good, I've got a buddy."

In my car on my next trip to New York, I took along my tape recorder and my first stop was Gibson Station in Valley Stream. I lived 15 years in Valley Stream approximately ½ mile from the railroad crossing at Gibson Station and never heard a train horn. As we sat in the car a train approached. The arms at the street crossing went down and I started recording. The bells were

ringing, and I announced that the lights were flashing. The train
pulled into the station, passengers got on and off, and the train
moved across the street crossing. You could hear the clickety
clack of the train wheels. No horn.

Mayor Cavalier made arrangements with Representative Ron Sil-
ver that we go to Tallahassee, our State Capital, and meet with
a committee of the House of Representatives about the horn.
We drove and got there at 9 A.M. The meeting was for 11 A.M.
Mayor Cavalier suggested that we go see the Commissioner. I
asked, "Will he see us?" "Let's try." We went to the Commissioners' office, told the receptionist who we were. She summoned
the Commissioner from his back office. He was dressed immacu-
lately, suit, shirt and tie. He welcomed us into his office and asked
us please take a seat on the couch. He said,

"What can I do for you?"

"We'd like to stop the train horn."

"What! You can't do that!" he yelled.

He then went into a long 15-minute discourse of how important
it was to keep the horn. That he rode with the engineer in his cab
and saw the need. When he finished, I asked him,

"Can I play a tape for you?"

"Yes."

I played the Gibson Station tape for him. No horn. He said,

"So what?"

I took out the book from the Florida Railroad Administration for 1984. I read to him that Florida and New York each had over 7 million registered vehicles, that each had over 400 gate crossings, then I showed him the accident figures: 100 Florida, New York 35. He turned around to the man sitting in the rear of the room and said,

"You tell the Committee that we don't need a train horn."

We thanked him and left.

At the Committee meeting there were about 10 men sitting waiting for us. We played the tape and showed the figures. They asked the man who came with us what did the Commissioner say?

"We don't need the train horn."

They voted unanimously, "No horn".

Legislation was passed in the House. The Mayor and I waited.

About 2 months later the Senate passed no horn. The Governor signed it. The Mayor and I came before the County Commissioners. They agreed <u>no</u> horn 10 P.M. until 6 A.M. Signs were installed at protected crossings. The entire year of 1985 we had no horn at night. There were 7 moving and one standing accident without the horn.

HORN AGAIN

In January of 1986 Congressman Lehman called and said that without the horn there was an increase in accidents. We were to have a meeting. At the meeting we were overwhelmed by at least a dozen men in black, all of them very excited. Mayor Cavalier and I were given accident reports. After a while someone said that if there were a center median, they would stop the horn. I said to the Mayor, "that is safety, let's go along with it".

We left with a bunch of accident reports in our hands. They brought back the horn. When I got home, I opened up an accident report and saw right away that the accident occurred during the day, not at night. I then got a call from Mayor Cavalier, he found the same error on the part of the Feds. What should we do? We gave up. You cannot fight the Feds. No matter what you say, they have to win. The next year, at night there were 29 accidents. The Feds don't care. I called FEC. That is a Fed law, period. Not until this week (7/8/2019) do we have peace from the FEC and the new High-Speed Train. Now we finally have a quiet zone.

DADE COUNTY

MOVING ACCIDENTS 10 P.M TO 6 A.M. - FEC R/R
CROSSINGS 1975 THROUGH 1990

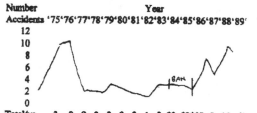

Number   Year
Accidents '75'76'77'78'79'80'81'82'83'84'85'86'87'88'89'

Total/yr   3   8   9   2   2   3   2   1   2 *3 *3**8 5 10 9

* **HORN BAN IN EFFECT FROM JULY 1984 THROUGH APRIL 1986** Miami – Dade County 29th – Miami-Dade County

****THE BAN WAS LIFTED IN APRIL 1986. THERE WERE 7 ACCIDENTS THAT YEAR ; TWO HAPPENED WHILE THE BAN WAS IN EFFECT, FIVE WHEN THE BAN WAS LIFTED**

YEAR	ACCIDENTS
75	3 (HORN) — NIGHT
76	8 "
77	9 "
78	2 "
79	2 "
80	3 "
81	2 "
82	1 "
83 started	2 "
84 - July 29 -	3 (Ban)
85	4 3 (Ban)
86 (Jan- May	2 (Ban)
86 June -Dec)	5 (HORN)
87	5 "
88	10 "
89	9 "

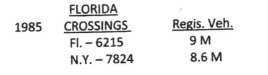

FLORIDA
1985   CROSSINGS   Regis. Veh.
              Fl. – 6215   9 M
              N.Y. – 7824   8.6 M

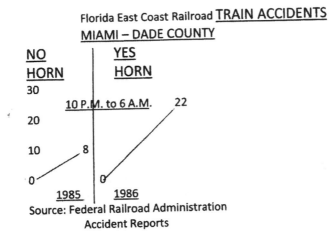

Florida East Coast Railroad TRAIN ACCIDENTS
MIAMI – DADE COUNTY

Source: Federal Railroad Administration
Accident Reports

WAHOO

I and three other guys went fishing on Seymours' boat. We hit into some dolphin. I had a line in the water and was starting to get rigged up on another rod for the dolphin when a young fellow said that my rod was bent. I went over, took it out of the holder, gave it a yank, and had on a big one. It was on my spinner with 20-pound test, so I had to play it carefully. It took a half hour to bring it in while the other guys watched me. The dolphins left. It was a 72-pound wahoo. We have a picture.

As you know, I enjoy going fishing. Naturally there are many stories which can be told but maybe I can tell a couple. I had bought a boat slip at Del Prado and finally got a twin engine inboard/outboard 24-foot cabin fishing boat. One trip at night brought in a lot of kingfish for both me and Eitan Schwarzbaum. Ready to go home, the engines wouldn't start. We called for help. The Coast Guard found us and gave our engines a boost. We got home but Margo was worried.

We were in New York when a hurricane hit. I got a call from Seymour; your boat is sunk. I rushed back and sure enough, it was under water. I found someone to put a sleeve under it, fill it with air, and raised the boat. The engines wouldn't start. The insurance company took it for $4,000.

I continued going fishing at Haulover on the party boats. One time I caught a huge fish at least 50 pounds which I gave the captain who said it wasn't kosher, in exchange for three Kingfish. Another time I got a hit which took the line and kept going until it stripped the reel. Goodbye line.

REBUILDING ISRAEL

One event I would like to include in this story. My father and I went to Philadelphia to visit our Lefkowitz cousins. They were in the candle business, the same as my father's parents were in in Lublin, Poland. As a youngster I met a cousin my age. He told me a story which he said he personally witnessed. It started when Rabbi Gershkenkorn returned from his second trip from Palestine. He wanted recruits to go to Palestine to B'nai Brock. My cousins and a few other families went with him. They did a lot of walking and came to a tree where they stopped to rest. Someone asked the Rabbi,

"When are we getting to Bnai Brock?"

"You're in Bnai Brock."

"What! Are you crazy?" they yelled.

"How can you bring us here to this desert with our children?"

"You are out of your mind."

They got a rope and put it around the Rabbi's neck. He told me he saw them do this. They stopped and took off the rope. The Rabbi became their first Mayor.

My 7th and last trip in Israel We got a taxi driver to take us to

B'nai Brock. I couldn't believe how busy the street was with pedestrians. Cars driving and stores were open on both sides of the street. I wanted to say my prayers, so I asked the taxi driver where to go. He pointed to a house and said that here they said prayers all day long. I should have no problem finding a room where prayers were being said. I went inside, said my prayers, and we left.

This 7th trip was started from a cruise ship on which I got sick, coughing all night. The doctor got me off the ship into a hospital the next morning in Haifa. Margo had 5 minutes to get our cabin emptied. She joined me. What a hospital experience. My bed was the first in a row separated by curtains. The bed to my right was quickly filled by a 90-year-old man coughing with pneumonia. I was given antibiotics and my food was Farina. Nurses were scarce so I was lucky that I had Margo as my advocate. The toilet was in the hallway, open to all. Margo got a cot and slept in the hallway. She wouldn't leave me. I stayed in the hospital 2 days when they sent me to a hotel. It was an old building being renovated. I got a nice clean room newly furnished. The hotel had a Kosher Chinese restaurant. The food was excellent, but I couldn't eat much. It was served in bowls over lit candles and you helped yourself with prongs in the bowls. Very nice. I had to stay in Israel for a certain amount of time after my illness before I was allowed to fly home.

LUCKY PHYSICAL TEST

One day my fishing buddy Dave called me. He was at the Veteran's Administration (VA) and they found an aortic aneurysm. He had to be operated on immediately because it could break and you're dead in a minute. The operation was successful, and he suggested that I also go to the VA and get it checked out. It won't cost me anything. He scared me so I went to the VA right away. Sure enough, they found that I had the same thing and got operated on immediately. That was luck. I had no symptoms to indicate a problem.

There were other operations I went through but before I went under the knife, I felt that Hashem was with me and I will be alright. And I survived them all. He must want me around is all I can say.

My eyesight was deteriorating so I went to Baskin Palmer, a well-known special eye hospital. It was a distance from where we lived and as a senior citizen I was entitled to STS, special transportation. I could have a companion. Arrangements had to be made at least 24 hours before pickup and return times.

A 2000 YEAR SHOCK IN EGYPT

As we were walking in Jerusalem, Margo says to me, "You know that we have come to Israel six times and we have seen everything. Let's go to Egypt."

"I said no", but she persisted.

As we walked, I saw a sign in a window which said Travel Agent, so I said let's ask. In the isle further back from where we walked in, sat a girl and a sign Travel Agent. We said that we wanted to go to Egypt. She said that we missed the bus. However, if we want, we can fly in. We agreed. Margo got her way. We arrived in Cairo and went to a hotel. They were full. We went to another hotel and asked for a low floor because it was Friday and we did not want to use an elevator on Shabbat. He put us on the second floor, but there were 7 floors below us for parking and offices. We awoke in the morning to the sound of car horns beeping. Looking out the small window it was dark. I opened the window and it was black outside. What was this black? I put my hand out the window and I could not see my hand. I took it back and asked Margo to do the same. She refused. I put my hand out again and again I couldn't see it. I took it back. The hand was not wet nor dirty. My hand was not damaged nor did any of the blackness enter the room. What is this blackness? Are we back to the time when the Egyptians had their plagues? We got dressed, walked the stairs down, had a hard-boiled egg for breakfast, and asked for directions to a synagogue. The man behind the desk gave us instructions on paper but since we could not carry on Sabbath, we tried to remember what he said. Miracle. We found the synagogue. The guard at the gate let us in and we walked over to a large building. Inside we were treated as guests. There were a large number of worshipers present.

The next day we went with a tour to the Cairo Museum. This museum was so huge that it housed another museum inside its premises. We walked throughout the museum and admired the artwork on the tombs and many other objects. We walked the length of the museum and then entered the smaller museum which was also huge.

Walking to the end we came to a window with a double table in front of it. We couldn't believe what we saw. On their haunches on the tables were two golden calves with about half the gold on each one removed. We were told that we were not allowed to take photographs and we didn't want to end up in an Egyptian prison. Maybe there will be a picture post card where we leave, but no luck.

Speaking to a fellow in synagogue at Del Prado who comes from Egypt, he was not surprised when I mentioned the Golden Calves.

We left Egypt by bus. It was not a pleasant ride through the desert. Why would anyone want to fight for this land? I remember as a child I used to hear it said that Israel land will remain vacant for

2,000 years and can only be restored by the Jews. It's amazing that that prophesy has come true.

RENTING A HOUSE

Walking on Main Street in Queens, New York, we saw a sign in a window to rent a house. Must keep Kosher. We inquired. This Rabbi owned a house and was going to the Catskill Mountains on vacation during the summer, 2 months.

"Do we keep Kosher?"

"Yes"

"I would like to speak to your Rabbi."

We gave him Rabbi Jungreis's phone number. The homeowner called us and said he will rent it to us. We moved in. If I saw something in the house out of place, I straightened it out, naturally. I'm always fixing things. After the two months in the house, as we are walking out the door, I got a piece of paper and wrote down 40 things that I fixed. The next year the Rabbi calls me up.

"Do you want to rent my house this year?"

"Why do you call me?"

"Where do you find a tenant who fixes up your house?"

"Yes, we will rent it again."

Again, I found about 35 things I fixed. A couple of years later while we were again on Main Street, it was Succoth time and we went to a restaurant which had a Sukkah outside. We brought our food outside and sat near a man who was already eating there. He looked very happy and said exuberantly,

"I just bought a house and it is in such perfect condition I can't get over it."

"Congratulations, where is the house?"

He described the house that we had rented.

BOUGHT A CO-OP IN QUEENS

At this time, we had also bought an apartment in Forest Hills, Queens from a friend we knew at Congregation Ohr Torah, Belle Ross. It was on the second floor, one bedroom and one bath. It had a large living room and bedroom. A wooden floor which I painted with polyurethane. I did the entire apartment. It was beautiful. The building was a co-op, six story, and a doorman. The outdoor black metal fence had some rust spots on it which I sprayed with Rust Reformer. I also sprayed the rusty legs at the bottom of the mailbox on the corner and the bottom of a street sign in front of the building. The mailbox attracted some graffiti artists, so I got some green paint from the post office and painted over the graffiti. Again, graffiti and again I painted it over right away. No more graffiti.

The synagogue I attended was a few blocks away, across Queens Blvd. It was an old building. Very few members. Prayer books were old and torn. I saw that I had work to do. I got the key to the building, which was very large, with a basement and balcony for women worshipers. I spent a lot of days working in the building, from roof to basement. I even asked the super at the apartment house to help me fix some leaks. The synagogue was in bad financial straits until I fixed the basement and we were able to rent it.

A few months later we sold our apartment to a young lady who just got an inheritance. She loved our apartment.

MYSTICAL EVENT (A REPEAT)

Could anyone in their wildest imagination have for seen the event in Stockholm, Sweden, when Margo and I were entering the front door of a train together with other passengers. As I got past the front seats, I saw other passengers in the car getting out of their seats and heading to exit by the middle door. I looked straight at a lady and she looked straight at me. People can live their whole lives and not encounter such an experience.

Margo standing, standing next to me, was astonished. Too bad we did not use our camera before she got off the train with other passengers directly behind her. What did we see?

WE SAW A MIRROR IMAGE OF MY OWN FACE

I still find it hard to believe, but Margo was a witness. How is this possible? Margo researched and found that the Swedes entered Poland many years ago. Now I asked Margo, "Do you remember the lady on the train?" "Of course, I remember. I'll never forget the resemblance, so perfect!".

FAMILY GENI

My family increased when Steven married Kim and they had a handsome son named Ben and a beautiful daughter named Molly. They are the apple of my eyes.

THESE ARE A FEW THINGS IN WHICH I PARTICIPATED

1- Brooklyn Technical High School -graduated top third

2- Pladmor Knitting Mills – learned manufacturing sweaters – repaired machines

3- U.S. Army – Infantry – 87 then 90th Division – Purple Heart

4- Knights of Pythias – Chancellor Commander – Sports chairman

5- Mighty Knitting Mills – Founder/President

6- Congregation Ohr Torah – 1974 N. Woodmere, N.Y. – First Treasurer

7- Congregation Ahavat Shalom – Queens, N.Y.

8- Urgent Construction – New York

9- Citizens Transportation Advisory Committee (CTAC) – Miami, Florida

10 -Project Whistle Stop – Co-President and founder – Stopped train horn Fl.

11 – Northeast Dade Coalition – after 4 years, 85 condominium members – President and founder

12 – United States Patent Office – 10/24/67 – new machine

13 – Kentucky Colonel

14 – Hineni of Florida – saved people from cults

15 – Platnick Realty – RE Broker – License # BK 0339064

16 – Community Awareness Forum of Del Prado – President and founder. Invited interesting speakers

17 – Jewish War Veterans – Miami, Fl. –   Invited interesting speakers

ADDENDUM

COMMON SENSE COMMENTS

<u>Information from my father</u>:

1- You cannot watch a crook, a crook watches you.

2- His factory being in Little Italy, he told me, "You see nothing, you hear nothing, and you say nothing."

3- Since I was commuting from Brooklyn, he told me to never sit next to a woman, you never know what they could claim.

4- He said that he would rather make $25 a week working for himself than $50 working for someone else.

5- Settle disagreements without legal help. Compromise.

INFORMATION FROM ME

A. Joseph Platnick a/k/a Avraham Yosef ben Yitzchak (Hebrew name)

1- Never tell a lie, no matter what. Silence is best.

2- Never talk badly about anyone nor listen to critical speech about someone.

3- Moses was in the cleft of the rock when Hashem placed His hand over the cleft and walked past Moses who was 6 feet tall, Hashem showing only His back. Mathematically, could Hashem be 72 feet tall?

4- Jacob gave 3 flocks of animals to Esau as a peace offering. Is this an example we could follow nowadays when we release a prisoner?

5- Why do women live longer than men? Sitting at a large round table at a dinner for Holocaust survivors, we were 4 men to 8 women. At home it struck me that the Code of Jewish Law requires us to live where there is clean air and water. What activity is different between men and women? I can think of only one, that when a woman goes to the toilet, she sits. A man stands, thereby inhaling rising fumes. Now I make it a practice to turn my head to the side as I stand.

6- How to keep a large quantity of fish fresh? Bobby Nestler taught me: Cut up the fish in portions. Place in separate containers. Fill with water. Place in freezer. Any fish protruding will turn brown. Will be fresh for years. No smell.

7- Wet basement wall? Fill in cracks with Water Plug, cover with ThoroCoat (100% waterproof).

8- To get rid of Ant colony. Boric Acid & Honey.

9- To get rid of Mice. Mice poison covered with Honey.

10-   To keep half a can of paint from drying out, turn it up side down.

11-   Spray "Rust Reformer" on rusty metal.

12-   Leak? Look on your computer for proper sealant.

ADDITIONAL OCCURENCES

1- The owner and son of Walker Knitting Mills which was located nearby, came to see us at Pladmor. They asked if we could produce 200 dozen of a certain garment in 2 weeks. My father said yes as I was standing nearby. They asked that we sign an agreement. My father was ready to sign but the young man said "No, I want Joe to sign." I signed it and made sure that they got delivery on time. I couldn't believe that they trusted me.

2- Another similar incident occurred shortly after I was in business for myself. A salesman came and asked if we can produce 200 dozen sweaters for his buyer in 2 weeks. I said that I have one machine which can make what he wants, let me see if it is available. I came back and said that the machine is now busy, but I can put him up next week. He can get delivery in 3 weeks. He said, "No good." and started to leave. I said, "Wait a minute. Here is the office. Why don't you call you buyer and ask if they could take it in 3 weeks." He did just that and said 3 weeks is OK. He got delivery on time. It just shows that we can be honest.

3- An incident I still regret. I shook hands on a rental deal which I tried to retract but I couldn't find the man. Sorry. It still bothers me.

4 - <u>ACCIDENT INSURANCE</u>

A very important item, which I learned from Rabbi Theodore Jungreis many years ago

probably saved our lives in one instance when we skidded off the road at 60 miles/hour

into a forest.

Rabbi Jungreis told us that whenever we go on a long trip, to take along tzedakah (charity} money to be deposited at our destination. Since we will be on a Holy Mission, nothing harmful will happen to us. (That has proven to be the best insurance.)

VIRUS 5/1/20

"Why isn't there a penalty against persons who have the virus but do not go into isolation and treatment?

They are spreading the virus!"

A. JOSEPH PLATNICK

Events Keep Unfolding...

Dear reader, Enter below any occurrence which happened unexpectedly **to you**.

Made in the USA
Columbia, SC
14 November 2020